WITH

OPTICAL ILLUSIONS

By Eiji Orii and Masako Orii   Pictures by Kaoru Fujishima

Gareth Stevens Children's Books
Milwaukee

Weekly Reader Books offers several exciting card and activity programs. For information, write to WEEKLY READER BOOKS, P.O. Box 16636, Columbus, Ohio 43216.

This book is published by arrangement with Gareth Stevens Children's Books. Weekly Reader is a federally registered trademark of Field Publications.

Cover illustration by Carol White

Library of Congress Cataloging-in-Publication Data

Orii, Eiji, 1909-
    Simple science experiments with optical illusions / Eiji Orii and Masako Orii; illustrations by Kaoru Fujishima. — North American ed.
        p. cm. — (Simple science experiments)
    Includes index.
    Summary: Presents various optical illusions for the reader to perform which illustrate how visual perception can be distorted.
    ISBN 1-555-32853-9
    1. Optical illusions — Juvenile literature. [1. Optical illusions.] I. Orii, Masako. II. Fujishima, Kaoru. ill.
III. Title. IV. Series.
QP495.075 1988
152.1'48—dc19   88-24756

North American edition first published in 1989 by

Gareth Stevens Children's Books
7317 West Green Tree Road
Milwaukee, Wisconsin 53223, USA

This US edition copyright ©1989. First published as *Ate Ni Naranai Me (Let's Try Your Eyes)* in Japan with an original copyright © 1987 by Eiji Orii, Masako Orii, and Kaoru Fujishima. English translation rights arranged with Dainippon-Tosho Publishing Co., Ltd., through Japan Foreign-Rights Centre, Tokyo.

Additional text and illustrations copyright © 1989 by Gareth Stevens, Inc.

Series editor and additional text: Rita Reitci
Research editor: Scott Enk
Additional illustrations: John Stroh
Design: Laurie Shock

Technical consultant: Jonathan Knopp, Chair, Science Department, Rufus King High School, Milwaukee.

1 2 3 4 5 6 7 8 9 94 93 92 91 90 89

Every day, your brain tells you the meaning of something you see. You learn that certain patterns of lights and darks and lines mean that something is large or small, near or far, up or down.

But there are many patterns that you do not meet in nature. When you look at something entirely new, your brain tries to tell you it is like something that is already familiar. You can be fooled into thinking that you are seeing something that is not so. We call these confusing patterns optical illusions.

Lay a piece of thin paper over this page and trace the big star shown below. Inside of that star, trace and shade the smaller star. Put the book aside, and use a pencil to draw around the smaller star. That's not too difficult, is it?

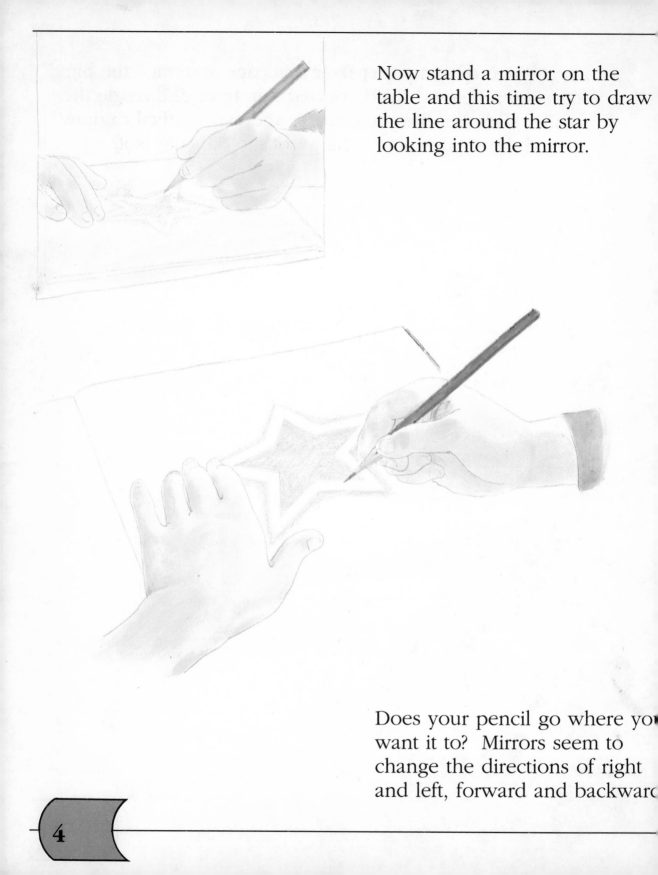

Now stand a mirror on the table and this time try to draw the line around the star by looking into the mirror.

Does your pencil go where you want it to? Mirrors seem to change the directions of right and left, forward and backward

On another piece of paper, draw a twisted path like the one on this page, with a starting point and a stopping point. With a pencil, trace the path from start to stop. Isn't that easy?

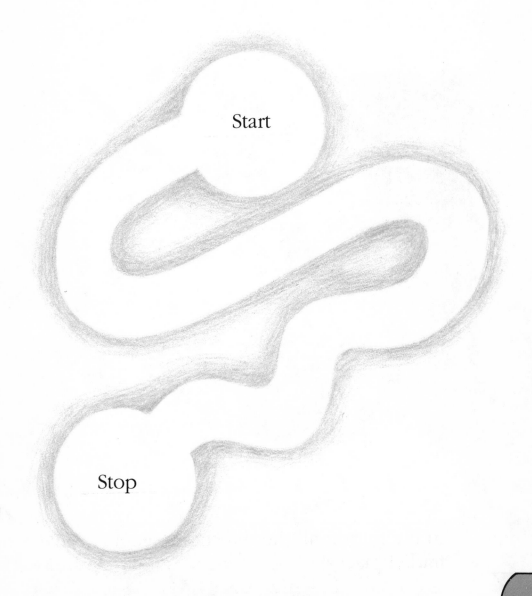

Start

Stop

Now put your drawing in front of a mirror. Place a stack of books in front of you so you cannot see your drawing. Try to trace the path just by looking in the mirror.

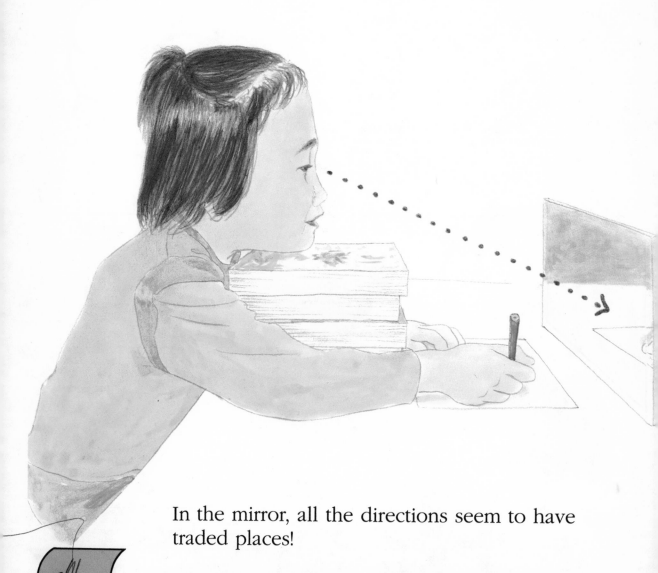

In the mirror, all the directions seem to have traded places!

Draw a big "69" on a piece of paper and put the paper on the wall. Now bend over and look at it through your legs. What do you see?

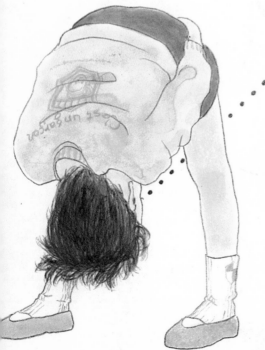

What happens if you turn the paper upside down and again bend over to look at it through your legs?

Someone seems to have gotten into the cake. Now turn the book upside down.

How did that piece of pie get there?

Here is a picture of a duck with little wings. What do you see when you turn the book sideways, with the duck's bill pointing to the ceiling?

Stand a postcard or a small piece of cardboard on the line between the butterfly and the flower. Then place your face down over the card. Look at the butterfly with your right eye as you look at the flower with your left.

What happens?

The butterfly seems to move closer to the flower.

Close your left eye. Hold up your index finger and line it up with a distant tree. Now open your left eye and close your right eye. What happens?

When you look out of your right eye, the tree appears to be lined up with your finger.

But when you look out of your left eye, the tree seems to have moved to the left.

Each eye sees a thing at an angle that's a little bit different from the other eye's view. This is how we see things as solid instead of flat.

Roll up a piece of paper into a tube and hold it to your left eye. Look through it at the things in front of you. Then place your right hand next to the paper tube, with the palm facing you. Now what happens when you look straight ahead?

Remember to look straight ahead with both eyes open.

Isn't that odd? It's as if you are looking through a hole in the palm of your hand!

What happens when:

you close your right eye?
you close your left eye?
you move your palm up, down, forward, and backward?

What do you see?

Because each eye sees a slightly different view, we can play these optical illusion tricks.

Stretch your arms in front of you and put your fingertips together. What happens when you look at your fingertips as you bring them closer to your eyes?

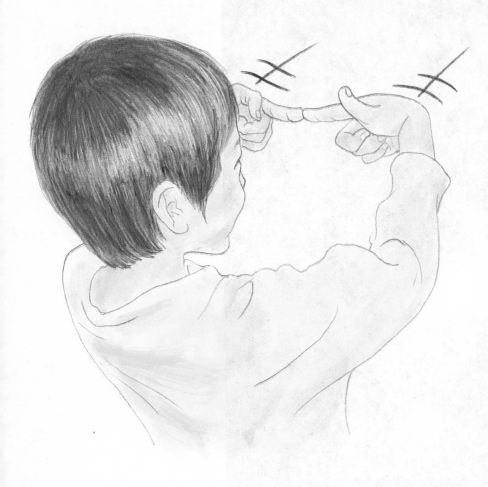

Your fingers look
like sausages!

Fireworks make
beautiful designs
in the evening sky.
You can, too.

Get a flashlight. Turn it
on and whirl it around in
the dark for your friends.
What will they see?

They will see a circle
because our eyes hold the
light image for a while.

Get a piece of cardboard and punch a hole through each end. Draw a goldfish on one side and a fishbowl on the other side. Loop rubber bands through the holes. Then twist both of the rubber bands tightly. Now pull on the ends of the rubber bands so that they untwist and the pictures whirl. What do you see?

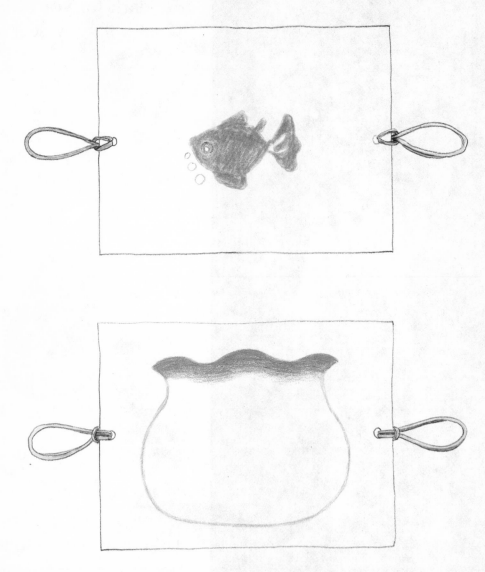

The goldfish is swimming in the bowl!

Our eyes hold a moving image a little bit longer than it takes for the image to move past.

Cut a piece of cardboard in the shape of a triangle. Put a pencil tip or toothpick through the center. Now spin it. What do you see?

Now cut a piece of cardboard in the shape of a square. Put a toothpick or pencil tip through the center and spin it. What does the square look like as it spins?

We see a circle because our eyes hold the image of the corners as they spin around.

Draw four lines on your cardboard square and spin it again. What kind of design do you see?

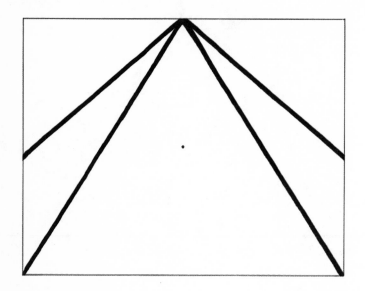

Draw two squares side by side that are exactly the same size. Now draw a bigger square around one and a slightly smaller square around the other. Do the first squares still seem to be the same size?

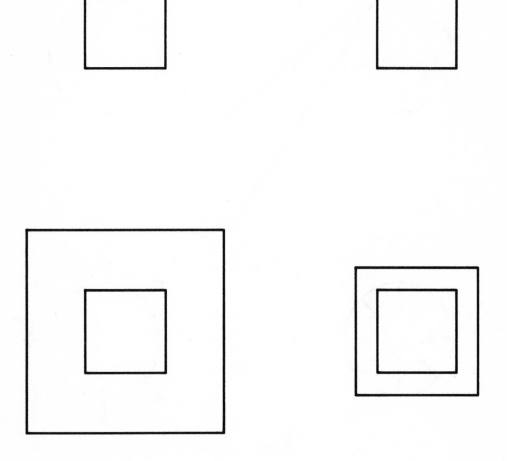

Our eyes are often fooled by the extra lines and shapes around the things we are looking at.

Using a large coin or a small glass or lid as a guide, trace two circles side by side. In one circle, draw some arrows pointing inside. Around the other circle, draw arrows pointing outside. Which circle now seems bigger?

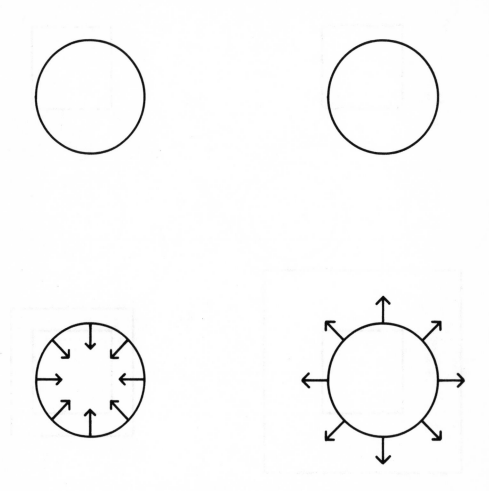

Different kinds of lines can make the same object look bigger or smaller.

Which circles on this page are the same size?

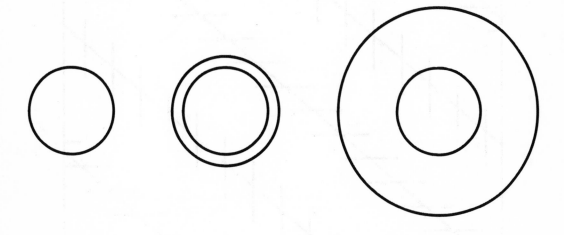

Now measure them with a ruler. Did you guess right?

Are the five slanted lines parallel to each other? Pick out which long lines slant exactly the same way.

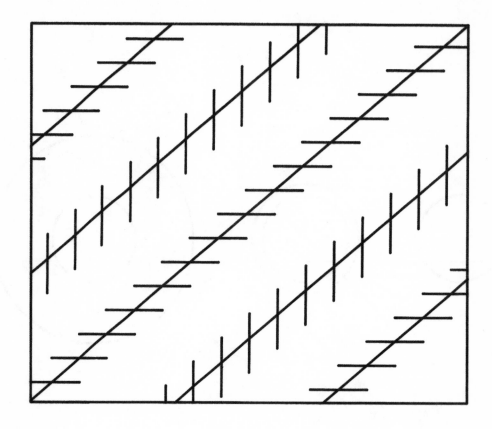

Now lay a ruler along one of the corner lines and carefully slide it to each of the other lines. Are you surprised?

Are the two red lines parallel to each other?

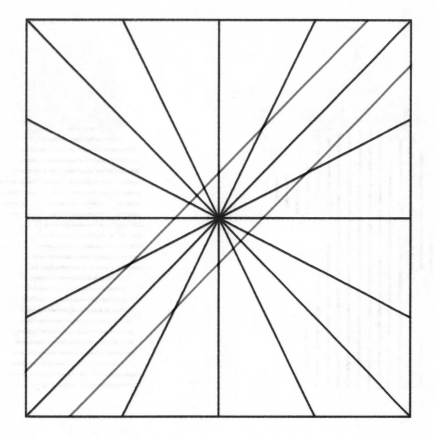

Lay two rulers, or two long pieces of paper, along the lines so that they go beyond the picture.

Is one of these girls taller than the other? Which one?
What do the lines tell your eyes?

Now measure each girl.

The figures drawn below are all the same size. In the bottom picture, the slanting lines of the background make us think that the two figures on the right are farther away. This tells our brain that they look smaller than when standing next to the figure on the left. So our brain decides that these big fellows would be even larger if they stood closer!

Because we really "see" with our brain, we have the fun and mix-ups of optical illusions.

GLOSSARY

Here is a list of words used in this book. After you read what each word means, you can see it used in a sentence.

design: a pattern, a picture
There are flowers in the design.

index: something that guides or points out
The index finger is sometimes called the pointer.

optical illusion: something you see that fools your brain into thinking it is something else
He thought he saw water on the road ahead, but it was just an optical illusion.

parallel: evenly, or equally, spaced and never touching; lines are said to be parallel to one another if there is an equal distance between them all along their length, so that they never touch; circles, too, can be parallel, as can a row of evenly spaced trees
When we park alongside the curb, we are said to be parallel parking.

sausage: chopped meat with lots of spices wrapped in a casing
Do you want sausage or soup for lunch?

stack: a neat pile
The stack of wood is for the stove.

stretch: reach, spread out, lengthen
You will need to stretch to put the books on the top shelf.

trace: to draw, sketch, or copy
Trace this design on the piece of cardboard.

triangle: an object or a shape with three sides
In music class, I play the triangle. It has three sides made of metal that ring when I hit them.

twisted: curved, with turns and circles
The twisted path wound through the forest.

INDEX

arrows 26
brain 2, 31
butterfly 11-12
cake 9
cardboard 3, 5, 11, 20, 22, 23
circles 19, 23, 26-27
design 18, 24
duck 10
figures 31
fingertips 17

fireworks 18
flashlight 19
flower 11-12
girls 30
goldfish 20-21
image 19, 21, 23
index finger 13
mirror 4, 6
number 69 7-8
optical illusion 2, 31
paper tube 15-16

parallel 28, 29
pattern 2
pie 9
rabbit 10
sausage 17
squares 23-25
stack 6
star 3-4
tree 13-14
triangle 22
twisted path 5-6

WITH

WATER

By Eiji Orii and Masako Orii   Pictures by Kaoru Fujishima

Gareth Stevens Children's Books
Milwaukee

Library of Congress Cataloging-in-Publication Data

Orii, Eiji, 1909-
    Simple science experiments with water / Eiji Orii and Masako Orii; Kaoru
Fujishima, ill.
         p. cm. — (Simple science experiments)
    Includes index.
    Summary: Presents experiments demonstrating the buoyancy of water.
    ISBN 1-555-32859-8
    1. Archimedes' principle—Experiments—Juvenile literature.
[1. Archimedes' principle—Experiments. 2. Floating bodies-
-Experiments. 3. Water—Experiments. 4. Experiments.] I. Orii,
Masako. II. Fujishima, Kaoru, ill. III. Title. IV. Series.
QC147.5.O75   1989   88-23304
532'.2—dc19

North American edition first published in 1989 by

Gareth Stevens Children's Books
7317 West Green Tree Road
Milwaukee, Wisconsin 53223, USA

This US edition copyright © 1989. First published as *Ukishizumi (Let's Try Buoyancy)* in Japan with an original
copyright © 1988 by Eiji Orii, Masako Orii, and Kaoru Fujishima. English translation rights arranged with
Dainippon-Tosho Publishing Co., Ltd., through Japan Foreign-Rights Centre, Tokyo.

Additional text and illustrations copyright © 1989 by Gareth Stevens, Inc.

Series editor and additional text: Rita Reitci
Research editor: Scott Enk
Additional illustrations: John Stroh
Design: Laurie Shock
Translated from the Japanese by Jun Amano
Technical consultant: Jonathan Knopp, Chair, Science Department, Rufus King High School, Milwaukee

2 3 4 5 6 7 8 9 9 94 93 92 91 90 89

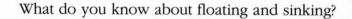

What do you know about floating and sinking?

Did you ever start to sink when you were swimming? And
did someone show you how to float? If so, you already kne
something about sinking and floating.

Some light things can sink and some heavy things can float.
The same object can sink at times or float at other times. T
experiments described in this book will help you find out
more unexpected things about how water makes things sin
and float.

Look at all these vegetables! Can you guess which ones
will float and which ones will sink?

Fill a sink or a pail with water. Carefully place different fruits and vegetables in the water to find out which ones sink and which ones float.

If you put a raw egg in a glass of water, it will sink.

But some eggs float. Why?

Put one teaspoonful of salt into the water and stir. What happens if you add another teaspoonful of salt? How about if you add even more?

Gradually the egg begins to rise.

How many spoonfuls of salt do you need in order to get the egg all the way to the top of the water?

Salt water is heavier than fresh water. It will hold up more weight. This is why things float more easily in salt water.

Ask an adult for a one-quart (one-liter) bowl. Fill it with water and add four tablespoons of salt. Stir until the salt dissolves. Now carefully put three or four raw eggs in the water. Do they float? Add enough salt to make the eggs float. Which end is up? Can you guess why?

An egg floats with the bigger end up because on that end there is a pocket of air inside the shell. This makes the egg light on that end. As eggs get older, the air pocket gets larger, so you can tell when eggs are fresh. Fresh eggs will not float to the top as easily as the older ones.

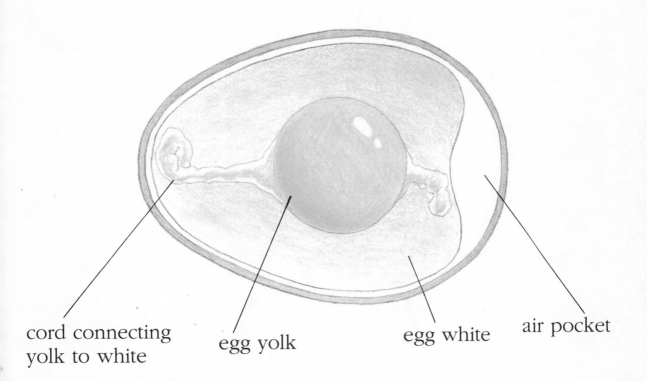

cord connecting
yolk to white

egg yolk

egg white

air pocket

Try using sugar instead of salt to make your egg float.
Add sugar a tablespoon at a time.

How about using soy sauce? Does the soy sauce make the egg float?

Put a raw egg into a glass of vinegar. What do you see?

Calcium is a mineral that makes bones, teeth, and shells strong. Vinegar is a weak acid. The vinegar combines with the calcium in the eggshell and produces bubbles of carbon dioxide gas.

The bubbles surround the egg and float it up to the top.

Keep the egg in vinegar overnight. Is it still floating? The shell is soft because most of the calcium has been taken out by the vinegar.

Try leaving a grape in a light-colored soda overnight.

When the grape is covered with bubbles, it will float. The bubbles are carbon dioxide gas from the soda. This gas is what makes the soda fizz.

Try the same experiment with a raisin and a button.

A gigantic tanker sails on the sea.

Why does such a huge steel tanker float while a small vegetable, such as a potato or a carrot, will sink?

Fill a large bowl with water. Get two pieces of aluminum foil about 3 x 6 inches (8 x 15 cm) each. Crumple up one piece into a large loose wad. Carefully set the crumpled wad on the water. What happens?

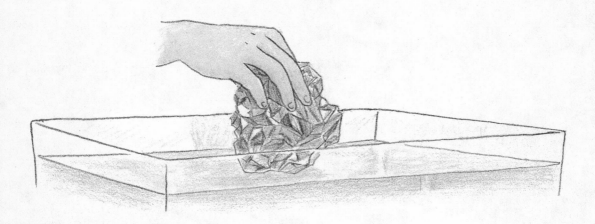

Fold and roll the other piece of foil as tightly and as small as you can. Then place the tightly rolled aluminum on the water. What happens now?

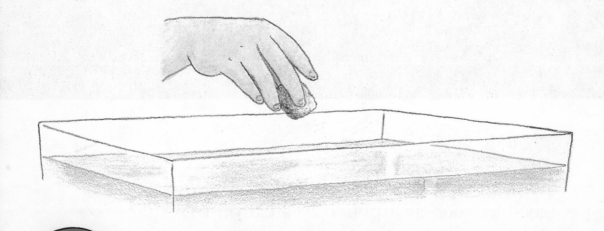

The large crumpled ball floats. It is spread out over a large area of water.

The small tight roll sinks. This is because it covers a much smaller area of water.

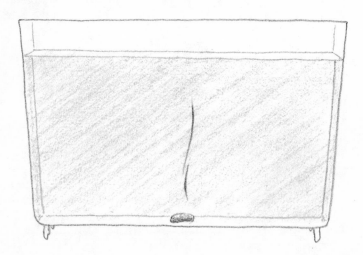

Get some plastic or rubberlike putty or clay that won't break up in water. Pack it into a solid ball and place it on the water. What happens?

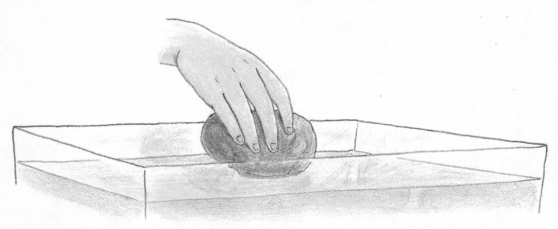

Now shape the same amount of clay or putty into a boat. Be sure there are no places where water can come through. Carefully set your boat on the water. What happens this time?

The small putty ball takes the place of just a little water. This little amount of water weighs less than the ball. So the putty ball sinks.

The putty boat takes up, or displaces, much more water. The amount, or volume, of water it displaces weighs as much as the boat. So the boat floats.

Gently place a cup right side up on the water. What happens?

Now turn the cup upside down and place it on the water.
What happens now?

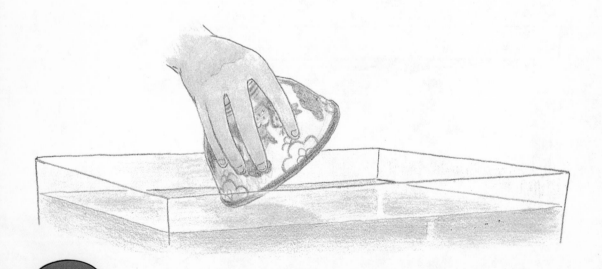

The upright cup floats.

The upside-down cup sinks.

Some things will float or sink depending upon how they sit in the water.

Get two metal washers of the same size. Hang them on the ends of a small stick or pencil with thread or thin string. Tape the thread in place on the stick. Tie a flat shoelace to the middle of the stick. Slide the shoelace back and forth until the stick stays level when you hold it by the shoelace. You may want to ask an adult to help you with this.

Hold the stick level and lower one of the washers into a glass of water. What happens?

Why does the stick tip up on one end? Has the weight of the washers changed? Is something helping to hold up one of the washers?

Now try putting both of the washers into the water. What happens this time?

The water in each glass helps hold up the same amount of weight in each washer. This is what makes the stick become level again.

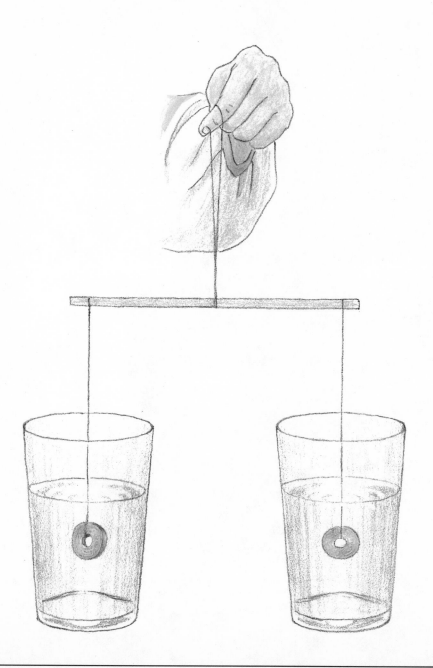

Put some salt into one of the glasses and stir. Then lower the washers into the glasses the same way that you did before. What happens?

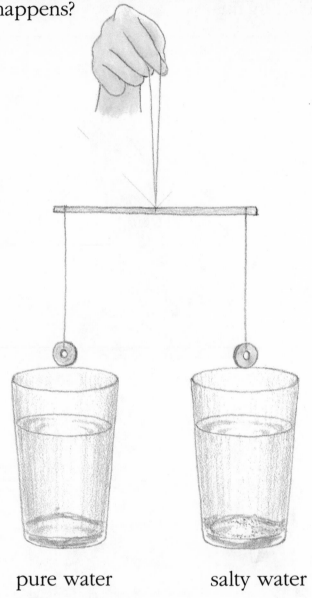

pure water   salty water

Does the salty water hold up more of the washer's weight this time?

pure water salty water

Make two balls of clay or putty. One should be loosely rolled and the other should be tightly packed. Tie both balls to the ends of a stick. Loop a flat shoelace around the stick, and slide it to a place where the stick will hang level. Tape the shoelace in place. Fill two glasses with water. What happens when you lower both balls into water at the same time?

Which ball seems to be lighter in water — the bigger one or the smaller one?

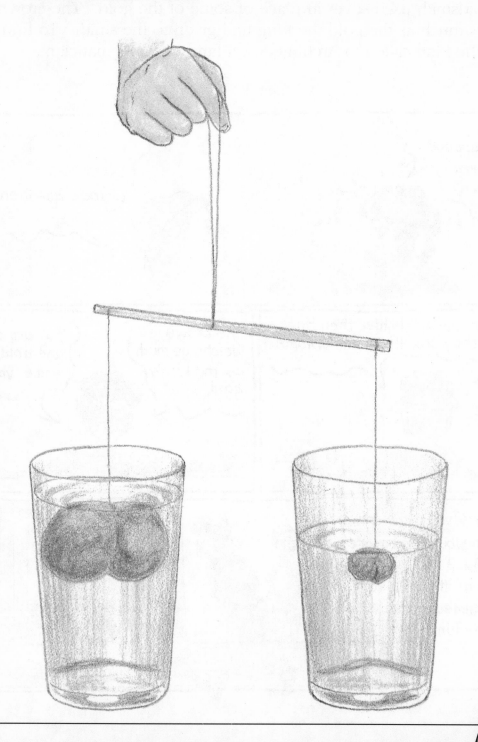

Archimedes and the Crown

Over 2,000 years ago, a Greek king ordered a gold crown. Later, he heard that the goldsmith used silver in place of some of the gold. The crown weighed as much as the gold the king had given to the smith. To find out the truth, the king called in Archimedes, a famous mathematician.

But one soak didn't do it. Archimedes thought for days. Then one day, as he got into his bath, he finally understood. Archimedes was so excited that he rushed into the street without his clothes!

Archimedes had discovered this law: When you sink an object in water, it takes the place of a volume of water that is the same as the volume of the object. The crown displaced too much water.

GLOSSARY

Here is a list of words used in this book. After you read what each word means, you can see it used in a sentence.

Archimedes: a Greek mathematician and inventor who lived from about 287 to 212 BC
The king asked Archimedes to find out if the smith used any silver when he made the gold crown.

area: a part of any surface
The children cleaned up the mess in the play area.

calcium: an important mineral that is found in foods and needed by both humans and animals to build strong bones and teeth
Birds need calcium to form the shells of their eggs.

carbon dioxide: a gas which leaves the lungs in breathing; needed by plants in making their food; used in soda water and fire extinguishers
The fizz in soda water comes from carbon dioxide gas.

displace: to take the place of

The ship will displace more than 10,000 tons of water.

gradually: little by little, slowly
She's gradually learning her multiplication tables.

mathematician: a person who studies how numbers work
She wants to be a mathematician when she grows up.

vinegar: a sour liquid with a strong odor, used in pickling foods and in salad dressings
She put vinegar in the potato salad to make it tangy.

volume: size, amount, bulk, quantity
A baseball has greater volume than a marble.

washer: a flat disk or ring of metal that is used to keep screws tight
He put a washer under the head of each screw.

INDEX

aluminum foil 16, 17
Archimedes 30-31
calcium 12-13
carbon dioxide 12-14
clay 18, 28
cup 20, 21
egg 5-13
grape 14
putty 18-19, 28

salt 5-8, 26, 27
soda 14
soy sauce 11
stick 22-27, 28, 29
sugar 10
vegetables 3, 4
vinegar 12, 13
volume 19, 30, 31
washers 22-27

WITH

STRAWS

By Eiji Orii and Masako Orii   Pictures by Kimimaro Yoshida

Gareth Stevens Children's Books
Milwaukee

Library of Congress Cataloging-in-Publication Data

Orii, Eiji, 1909-
    Simple science experiments with straws / Eiji Orii and Masako Orii;
Kimimaro Yoshida (ill.). — North American ed.
        p. cm. — (Simple science experiments)
    Translated from the Japanese.
    Includes index.
    Summary: Presents experiments using straws, cards, and glasses to
demonstrate the pushing force of air.
    ISBN 1-555-32854-7 (lib. bdg.)
    1. Atmospheric pressure—Experiments—Juvenile literature.
[1. Atmospheric pressure—Experiments. 2. Experiments.] I. Orii,
Masako. II. Yoshida, Kimimaro, ill. III. Title. IV. Series.
QC885.075 1989
507'.8—dc19   88-23298

North American edition first published in 1989 by

Gareth Stevens Children's Books
7317 West Green Tree Road
Milwaukee, Wisconsin 53223, USA

This US edition copyright ©1989. First published as *Nihon No Sutoro (Let's Try Straws)* in Japan with an .
original copyright © 1987 by Eiji Orii, Masako Orii, and Kimimaro Yoshida. English translation rights arranged
with Dainippon-Tosho Publishing Co., Ltd., through Japan Foreign-Rights Centre, Tokyo.

Additional text and illustrations copyright © 1989 by Gareth Stevens, Inc.

Series editor and additional text: Rita Reitci
Research editor: Scott Enk
Additional illustrations: John Stroh
Design: Laurie Shock
Translated from the Japanese by Jun Amano
Technical consultant: Jonathan Knopp, Chair, Science Department, Rufus King High School, Milwaukee

2 3 4 5 6 7 8 9 9 94 93 92 91 90 89

Every day you go through air so easily that it does not seem
as if there is anything at all to air. Sometimes we even call it
"thin air."

But air has weight and force. Moving air is wind. Air takes
up room. Air rushes into empty spaces. Air can push heavy
things, or keep some things from moving at all.

With the help of drinking straws and some other everyday
things, you can see for yourself some of the amazing things
air can do.

Put a drinking straw in a glass of water and sip.

When you take away the air in the straw, the air pressing on the water in the glass outside the straw quickly forces some of the water up the straw to fill the empty space.

Will you get more water sipping through one straw or two?

You get more water through two straws.

You lower the air pressure in two straws. Air pushes from high pressure to low pressure. It pushes the water up both straws.

Now take one straw out of the glass and try to sip through both straws at once. What happens?

Only a little water comes up.

The air you take out of the first straw is at once replaced by air from the second straw. Water is not forced up the straw in the glass because the air pressure is the same in the straw as on the water.

What happens when you put your fingertip over the end of the straw that is out of the glass?

Now water comes up easily, just as when you used only
one straw.

Try this with straws of different sizes.

Now let's try this with three straws. Put two straws in the glass and one outside the glass. Then sip. What happens?

If you put your fingertip over the end of the straw and sip,
what happens?

Now see what happens when you leave one straw in the glass and put the other two outside.

Put your fingertip over the end of one of those straws and then sip. What happens?

Try covering the ends of both straws and sipping. What happens? For water to move, air must be able to push it.

Fill a soda bottle with water up to the top. Put a straw in the bottle and plug up the rest of the opening with clay or putty. Be sure no air can get through the plug. Can you sip water through the straw?

No, you can't. There is no air in the bottle to push the water up the straw.

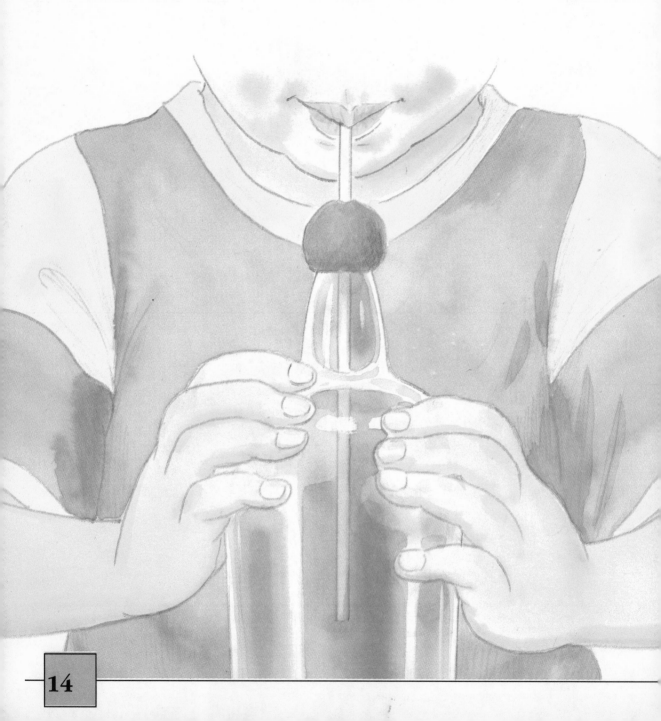

Find out what happens when you sip on two straws, one in the bottle and one outside.

The water still can't come up.

Now put the two straws in the bottle and carefully seal the opening with clay or putty. What happens when you sip on both straws?

Try sipping on only one straw. Does the air coming through the second straw push the water up?

Try this over a sink. Fill a glass with water, put a postcard on the glass, and hold it in place with your hand. Now turn the glass upside down and let go of the postcard. What happens?

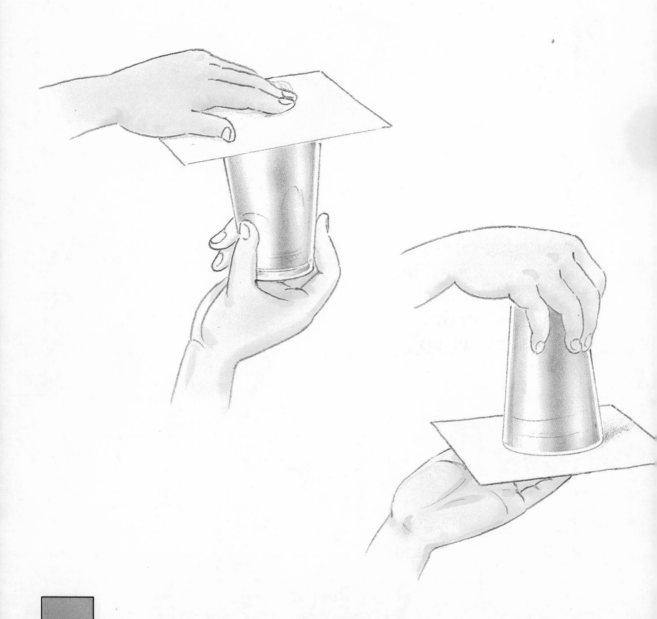

That's strange! The postcard doesn't fall. Why not? Can air get inside to help the water come out?

Let's see if holes will help. Be sure to do this over
the sink! Make a small hole in the postcard with a pin.
Then turn the glass upside down. Now let go of the
postcard. Did it stay, or did it fall?

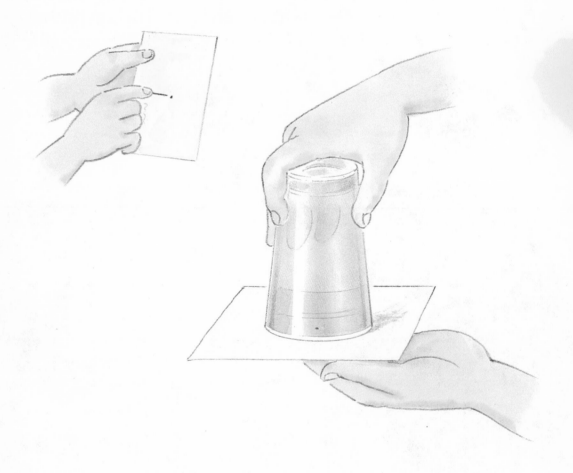

What happens when you make another small hole? Two
more holes?

Will lots of small holes let air in and water out?

In tiny holes, water forms a strong "skin" called surface tension. The air pressure against this surface tension is stronger than the weight of the water above. This air pressure holds up the postcard.

Now make larger holes. The bubbles show that air is getting inside the glass. Now the water can flow out, pushing away the postcard.

Using a can opener, make a very small hole in the top of a soda can close to the rim.

Now tip the can. Be sure to do this over the sink or a bowl!

Does the soda come out?

Now let's make another small hole in the can across from the first one.

This time, air can get in easily
to push the soda out.

Pour out all the soda and put the can into a pail or a large bowl filled with water. Be careful not to bend the can as you hold it under the water. What happens?

Air comes out of the can because air is lighter than water.

Take the can out of the pail and pour from it. Did water go in to fill the space left by the air?

Now empty all the water out of the can. Put your finger over one of the holes and hold the can under water.

Do bubbles come out?
Not many.

Try to pour. Not much water gets into the can. Most of the air stays inside.

Can air push out and water push in through the same small hole at the same time?

When you do the experiment on page 18, the postcard does not drop. Let's see what happens when the glass is not quite filled with water.

Fill the glass almost to the top and put the postcard on it.

Hold the postcard on the top.

Turn the glass upside down.

Take away your hand. The postcard does not fall.

Now let's see what happens when there is no water at all in the glass.

This time the postcard falls!

What if the rim of the glass is wet?
Dip the rim of the glass in water.

Press the postcard firmly on the glass
so the water seals it around the rim.

Now turn the glass upside down
and let go of the postcard.

The postcard does not fall.
The air pressure outside the
glass is higher than inside
the glass. The water seal
keeps more air from getting
inside the glass.

A plastic goldfish "swims" inside two glasses full of water and placed mouth to mouth. You can make this happen, too.

Here's how.

Get two glasses of the same kind and size. Fill one up with water and put a plastic fish or another floating toy in it. Fill the second glass to the brim and put a postcard on it.

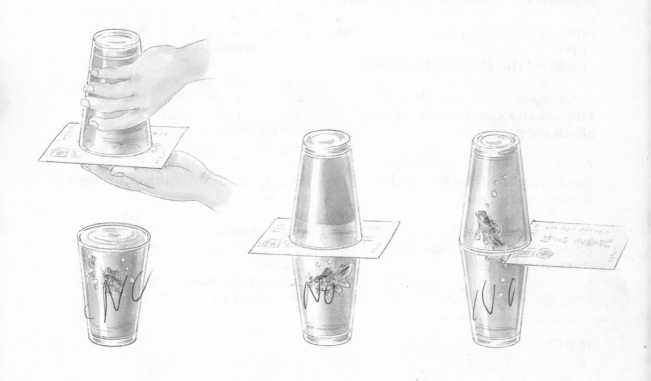

Turn the glass with the postcard upside down.

Set it on top of the other glass.

Keep the edges of the glasses close together while you pull out the postcard very carefully.

Now your plastic fish can "swim" happily in its aquarium!

GLOSSARY

Here is a list of words and phrases used in this book. After reading what the word or phrase means, you will see it used in a sentence.

air pressure: the weight of air against a surface. Higher air pressure means that the air is heavier than normal. Lower air pressure means that the air is lighter than normal.
At sea level, the normal air pressure is about 15 pounds per square inch.

brim: the topmost edge of a cup, glass, or bowl
She filled the glass to the brim.

experiment: a test, trial, or project
She did an experiment to learn about air pressure.

firmly: in a strong, steady way
She firmly held the bat as she waited for the ball.

plug: to stop up, or fill, a hole or a gap
Be sure to plug the sink before you wash the dishes.

rim: an edge or border of something
He swam to the rim of the pool.

seal: something that closes tightly to keep out air or water
His mother put a wax seal on each of the jars of jelly she made.

sip: to drink small amounts carefully
You have to suck the air when you sip through a straw.

straw: hollow stalks or stems of grain after the seeds have been removed; a single such stem used for drinking fluids; a drinking tube made of plastic, glass, waxed paper, or other material
He sipped his fruit juice through a straw.

surface tension: the strong invisible "skin" that forms over the surface of water
The surface tension let the insect run across the pond.

INDEX

air pressure 4, 6, 21
bowl 22, 25-26
brim 31
bubbles 21, 25-26
can opener 22, 24
clay 13-17
experiment 27
glass 3-12, 18-21, 27-31
goldfish 30-31
hole 20-22, 24, 26
pail 25-26
plug 13

postcard 18-21, 27-31
putty 13-17
rim 29
seal 17, 29
sip 3-17
soda bottle 13-17
soda can 22-26
straws 3-17
surface tension 21

WITH

CIRCLES

By Eiji Orii and Masako Orii   Pictures by Kaoru Fujishima

Gareth Stevens Children's Books
Milwaukee

Library of Congress Cataloging-in-Publication Data

Orii, Eiji, 1909-
    Simple science experiments with circles / Eiji Orii and Masako Orii;
Kaoru Fujishima (ill.). — North American ed.
       p. cm. — (Simple science experiments)
    Translated from the Japanese.
    Includes index.
    Summary: Presents experiments demonstrating properties of circles
and loops made of cloth, paper, and string.
    ISBN 1-555-32857-1 (lib. bdg.)
    1. Circle—Experiments—Juvenile literature. 2. Topology-
-Experiments—Juvenile literature. [1. Circle—Experiments.
2. Experiments.] I. Orii, Masako. II. Fujishima, Kaoru, ill.
III. Title. IV. Series
QA484.075 1989
507'.8—dc19   88-23295

North American edition first published in 1989 by

Gareth Stevens Children's Books
7317 West Green Tree Road
Milwaukee, Wisconsin 53223, USA

Series editor and additional text: Rita Reitci
Research editor: Scott Enk
Additional illustrations: John Stroh
Design: Laurie Shock
Translated from the Japanese by Jun Amano
Technical consultant: Jonathan Knopp, Chair, Science Department, Rufus King High School, Milwaukee.

2 3 4 5 6 7 8 9 9 94 93 92 91 90 89

Look at a plain circle. It seems to be a simple thing, doesn't it? But a simple circle can hide a lot of tricks! The rings, loops, and circles you'll read about in this book will help you learn more about patterns and shapes and some of the unexpected things they can do.

Cut a hole in a postcard. Now try
pulling the circle over your body.

It's impossible! Or is it?

Try it this way.

Fold a postcard in half the long way.

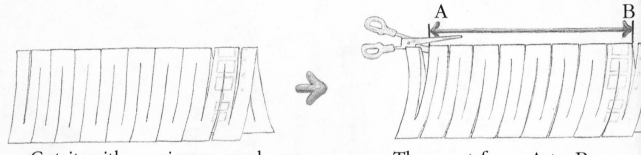

Cut it with a scissors as shown.   Then cut from A to B.

Unfold the postcard.

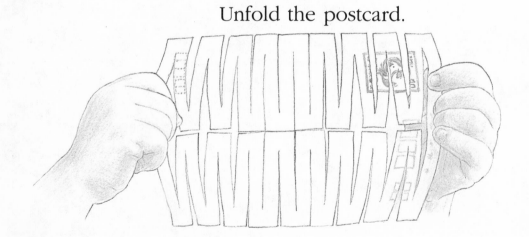

Now you can pull it down over yourself.

Get a piece of paper the same size as a business card. Fold it and cut it the way you cut the postcard. Now pull it over your head.

If you want a bigger loop, do you make your cuts closer together or farther apart? Use two pieces of paper the same size. Make the cuts on one very close together. Make the cuts on the other farther apart.

Put a penny on a piece of paper. Draw a line around the penny. Cut a hole in the paper, following the line of the circle you drew. Can you pass a quarter through the hole without tearing the paper?

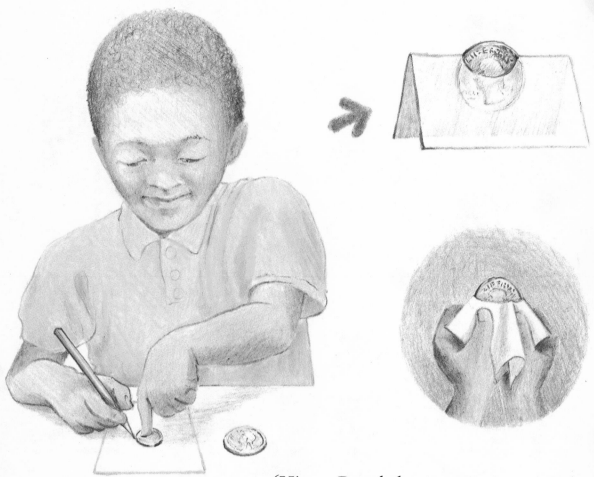

(Hint: Bend the paper very gently to ease the quarter through.)

The cut you made in the paper is big enough to fit over the quarter if you straighten the cut out first.

Try linking strips of cloth.

Cut four pieces of soft cloth. Make
each piece 2 inches (5 cm) wide
and 6 inches (15 cm) long.

Fold them together as shown.
Make holes in the centers as
shown by the dots below. Ask
an adult to help you make the holes.

What will happen if you
take the end of the cloth
and pull it through the
holes?

The pieces will be linked together!

Get a long piece of string, double it, and loop it through the handle of a cup. Hang the cup by the string on a rod or stick. Can you get the cup loose without untying or cutting the string?

Here's how.

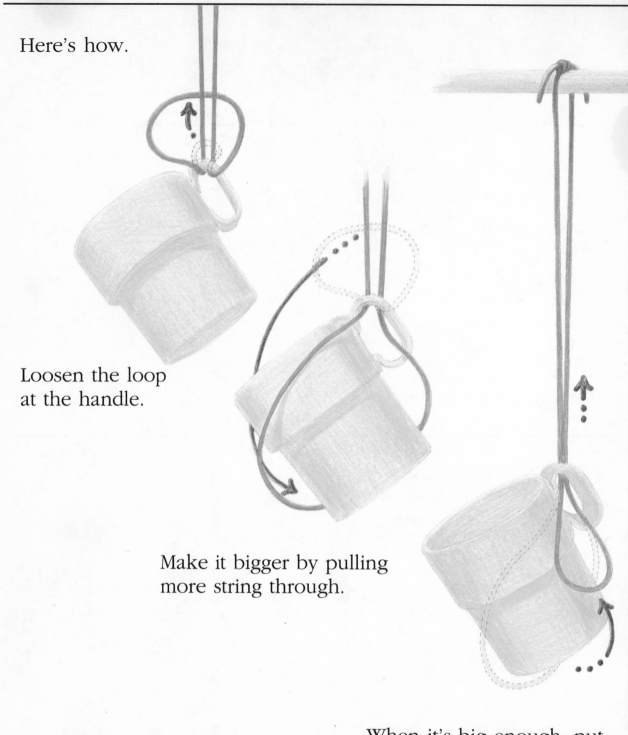

Loosen the loop
at the handle.

Make it bigger by pulling
more string through.

When it's big enough, put
the cup through the loop.

Make a circle with your thumb and index
finger. Have a friend try to break the circle.
This will be easy if your friend pulls your
circle apart with his or her index fingers.

But you can do it
so that the circle
will not break.

This time, when you make a circle with your index finger and thu[mb,] hold your other fingers back stiffly at eye level. Now ask your frie[nd] to try to break your circle with his or her index fingers.

Holding the other fingers out stiffly tightens the muscles in your hand. This helps clamp your index finger strongly against your thumb.

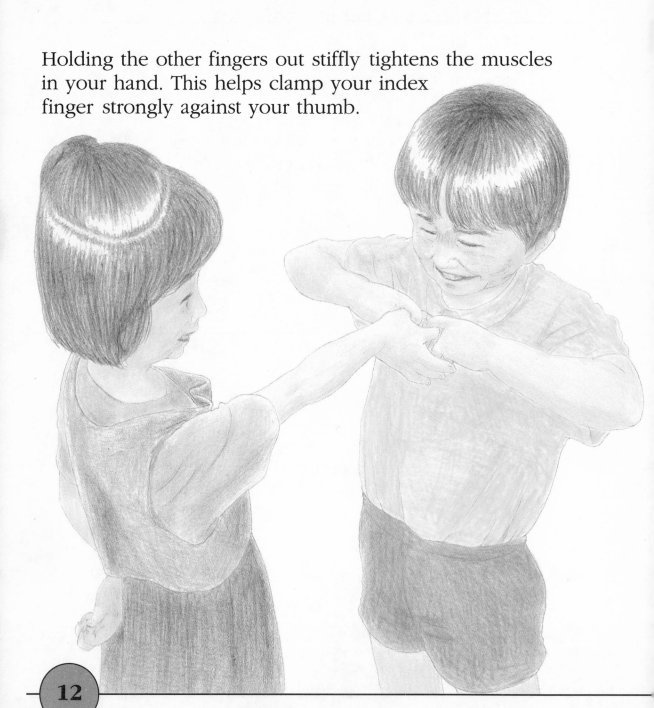

Tie a piece of thread into a circle. Fill a dish with water and lay the thread on the surface so that it floats. Does the thread form a perfect circle?

The surface of water tightens up to form a thin, firm "skin" that we call surface tension. The thread is held up on top by the surface tension of the water in the dish.

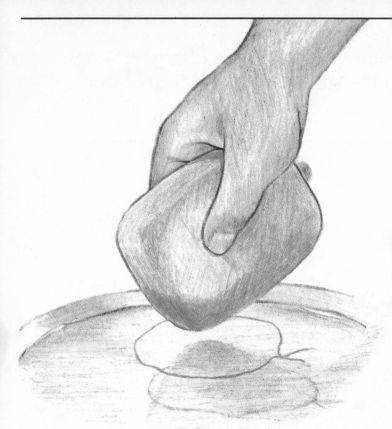

Touch the surface of the water inside the thread with a wet bar of soap. What happens?

Soap weakens the surface tension of water.
The water relaxes suddenly in all directions,
pulling the thread out into a perfect circle.

Try this using containers of different shapes.

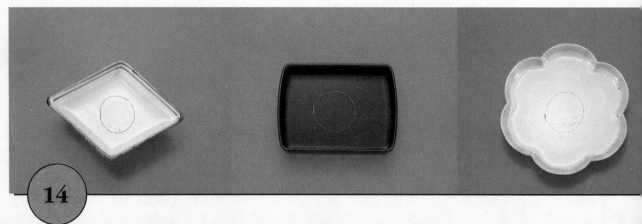

Make shapes from
apple skins.

Ask an adult to skin an apple in
one long unbroken strip.
What kind of shape will you
get if you put the skin on a table?

You will get this!

A loop-the-loop roller coaster will keep going as long as you are on it.

Try your own tricks with loops.

Cut a long piece of paper 1 1/2 inches (4 cm) wide. Tape both ends together to make a loop. Keep the strip straight when you do this.

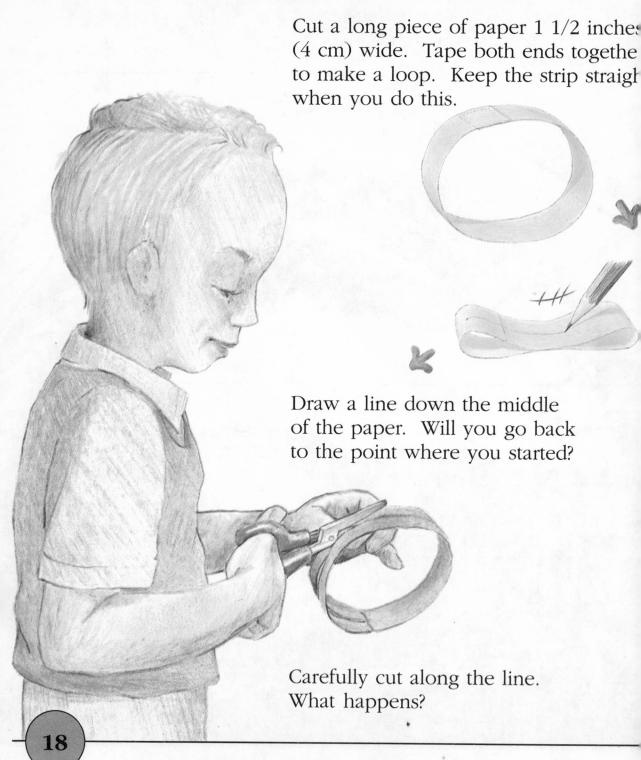

Draw a line down the middle of the paper. Will you go back to the point where you started?

Carefully cut along the line. What happens?

You will get two loops of paper.

Make a different kind of loop.

Cut another long strip of paper. But this time, twist the strip once before you tape the ends to make a loop.

Draw a line down the middle of the paper. What happens when you try to draw it back to the starting point? How many sides does this strip have?

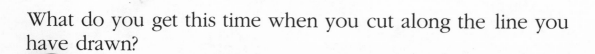

What do you get this time when you cut along the line you have drawn?

You get a bigger twisted loop!

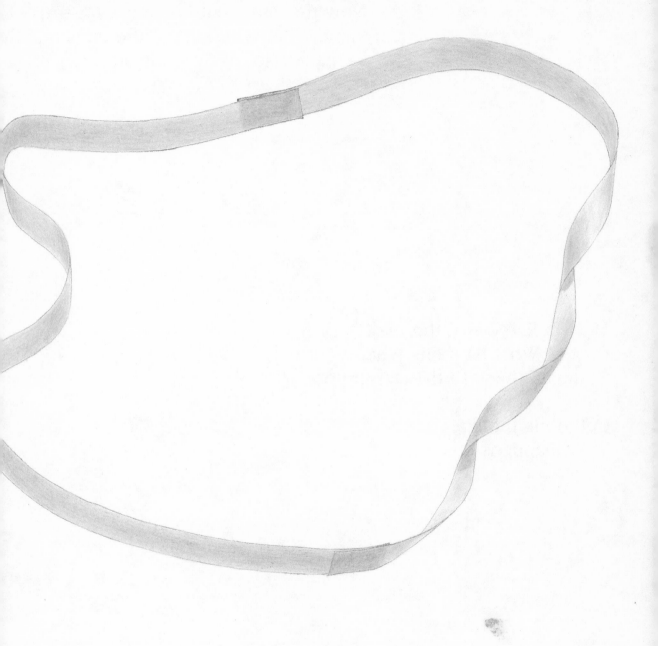

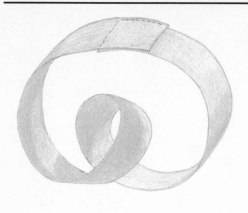

Try a double twist.

Now this time, cut another long strip of paper. Before you tape the ends togeth[e] to make a loop, twist the strip twice.

Draw a line down the middle of the paper. What happens when you try to draw it back to the starting point?

Cut along the line.
What happens this time?

You get two twisted loops linked together!

Now, cut a strip of paper and twist it three times. Tape the ends. Draw a line down the middle of the paper. Cut along the line. What happens?

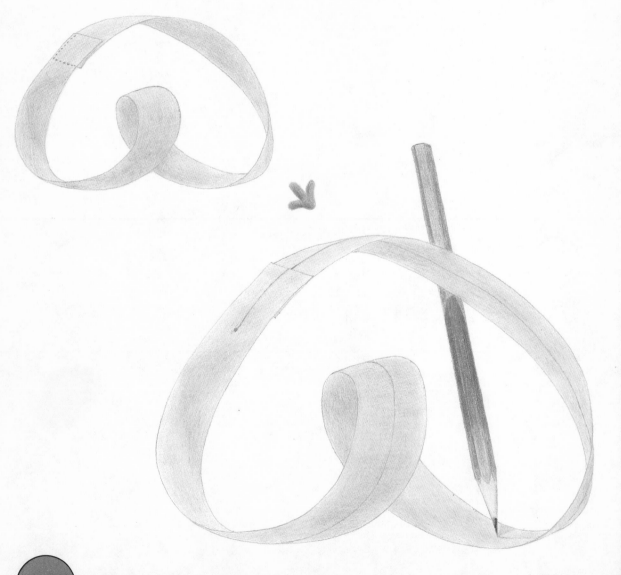

You get a twisted loop!

Try something a little bit harder.

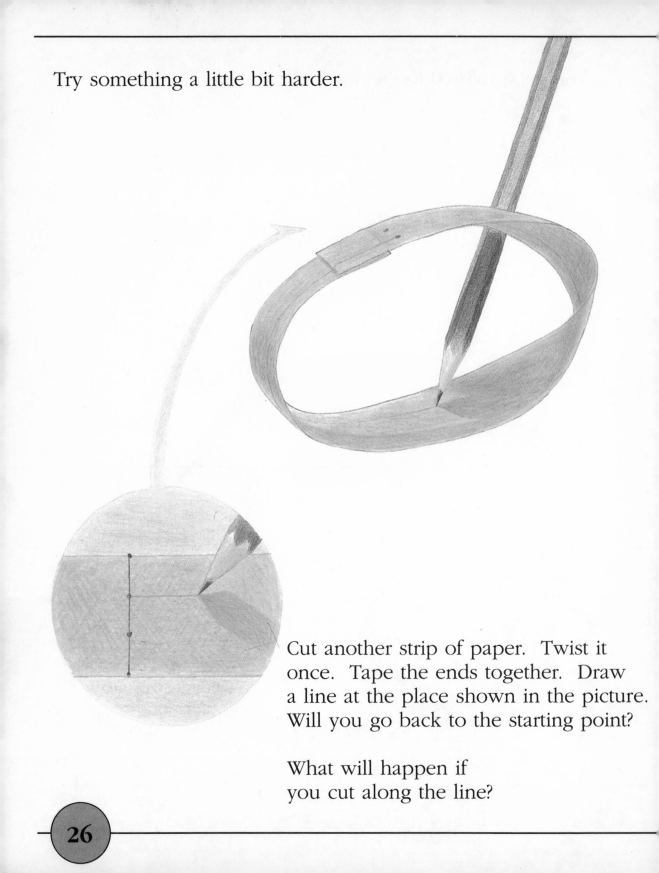

Cut another strip of paper. Twist it
once. Tape the ends together. Draw
a line at the place shown in the picture.
Will you go back to the starting point?

What will happen if
you cut along the line?

You get a twisted large loop and a twisted small loop linked together.

Let's tape two loops together.

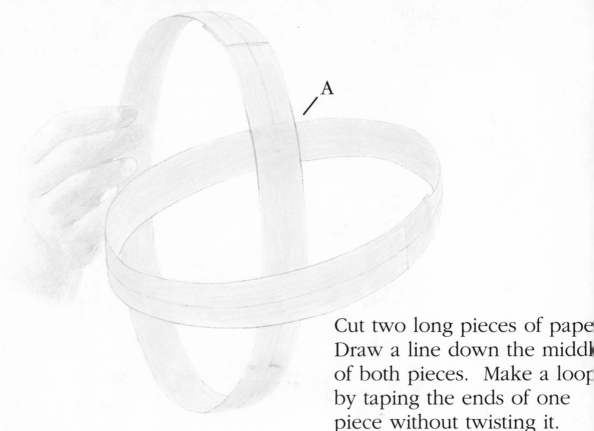

Cut two long pieces of pape
Draw a line down the middl
of both pieces. Make a loop
by taping the ends of one
piece without twisting it.

Put the other piece of paper through
the loop. Tape its ends to make a
loop, but don't twist it. Tape the
two loops together at the place
marked A.

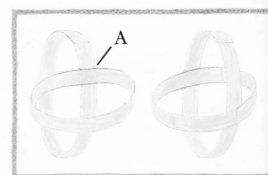

Cut along the line. What happens?

Try taping them in different way.

This time you get a large square!

How can rings be linked together, but still not linked together?

Look carefully at the drawing below. Is the blue ring linked to the red ring? To the white ring? Is any ring linked to any one other ring?

No, but you still cannot move the rings apart! What is holding the rings together? The next page will help you find out.

Make this puzzle. Cut out three rings. Color one red.
Color another one blue. Keep the last one white.

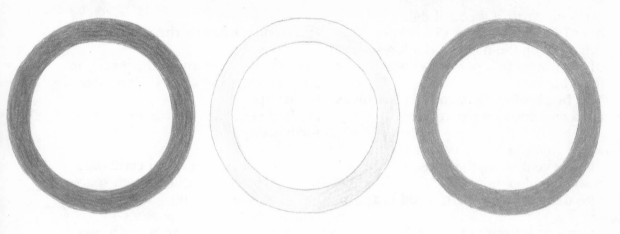

Lay the blue ring on the red one. Cut the white ring apart.
Pass the white ring through the blue ring and the red ring.
Follow the direction of the arrows in the drawing.

Tape the white ring back together. Now gently try to
remove one ring. See how they stay together? Now show
others the unexpected things circles can do!

GLOSSARY

Here is a list of words and phrases used in this book. After you read what each word or phrase means, you can see it used in a sentence.

business card: a piece of light cardboard 2 x 3 1/2 inches (5 x 9 cm) printed with the name and address of a business or a person who works for a business
The bookseller gave me his business card so I could write to him.

circle: a shape made by a line that bends evenly until the ends of the line come together
She drew a circle with a red crayon.

clamp: to grip or fasten tightly
Clamp the two pieces of wood together until the glue dries.

container: something that can hold liquids or solids
He put all the apples in containers.

index: something that guides or points something out
The index finger is sometimes called the pointer.

linked: connected or joined together
All the circles were linked into a single chain.

loop: a shape made by a line, a thread, or a piece of string that curves back so the ends touch
He made a loop in the rope.

loop-the-loop: an amusement ride on a metal track that makes a loop that stands upright
He had six rides on the loop-the-loop today.

postcard: a piece of light cardboard 4 x 6 inches (10 x 15 cm) with space for an address on one side and a written message on the other
My aunt and uncle sent me a postcard from Michigan.

ring: a small circular band of metal, plastic, or other material in a rigid shape; a mark in that shape
They played at tossing rings in the yard all afternoon.

surface tension: the tightly stretched surface of water; the tendency of water to round up into drops
The surface tension of the water let the insect run across the pond.

twist: to put a turn in a length of rope, paper, cloth, or other material
He twisted the towel to wring out the water.

INDEX

apple skin 15-16
business card 5
cloth strips 7-8
cup 9-10
finger circle 11-12

linked rings 30-31
paper loops 18-31
postcard 3-5
soap 14
square loop 29

surface tension 13-14
thread circle 13-14
three rings 30-31